ANIMAL LIFE STORIES

THE SQUIRREL

Kingfisher Books, Grisewood & Dempsey Ltd,
Elsley House, 24-30 Great Titchfield Street,
London W1P 7AD

First published in this edition in 1989
by Kingfisher Books
The colour illustrations in this book are
taken from *Eye View Library: The Squirrel*
originally published in hardback in 1976

BRITISH LIBRARY CATALOGUING IN PUBLICATION DATA
Royston, Angela
    The squirrel.
    1. Squirrels. For children.
    I. Title   II. Series
    599.32'32
ISBN 0 86272 454 6

Edited by Jacqui Bailey
Designed by Ben White
Cover design by David Jefferis
Cover illustration by Steve Holden/*John Martin & Artists Ltd*
Black and white illustrations by Jean Colville
Colour illustration on page 23 by David Cook
Phototypeset by Southern Positives and Negatives (SPAN)
Lingfield, Surrey
Printed in Spain

ANIMAL LIFE STORIES

THE SQUIRREL

By Angela Royston

Illustrated by Maurice Pledger

Kingfisher Books

The squirrel scampers down the pine tree. In winter she eats mainly the seeds of pine cones, but today she is going to search for buried nuts. She runs across the snow to the oak tree and scratches and sniffs until she finds an acorn. She grasps it in her paws and crunches it between her sharp teeth.

Darkness falls and the squirrel returns to her pine tree. She hears a fox prowling down below but she is not frightened. She wraps her bushy tail around herself and sleeps safe and warm in her drey made of twigs. Winter passes and at last spring comes. Now she finds young pine shoots to eat as well as cones. In the next tree a male squirrel watches her.

The female drops to the ground and the male squirrel bounds down after her. As she runs back to the trees, another male joins in the chase.

The branches shake as the squirrels leap from tree to tree until they are all tired out. Then the female squirrel stops and lets the first male come close to her and they mate.

It is nearly six weeks since the squirrel mated and her babies will soon be born. One day she pushes her nose into a dark hollow high up in the oak tree. A terrified starling flies out leaving three eggs in the nest. The squirrel breaks the eggs and licks up the food inside.

The squirrel decides the starling's nest will make a good drey. She fetches leaves, moss and twigs and packs them all around the hole. Then she pulls tufts of fur from her belly to make a soft floor.

The squirrel kittens are born next day. At first they are tiny creatures without any fur. They suck milk from their mother and sleep curled up to keep warm. Their mother leaves them only to find food.

By seven weeks the kittens are nearly fully grown.
They love to chase each other along the branches,
but they are still too young to go on the ground.
When one of them tries, their mother goes down and
half carries, half drags the large kitten back.

Now their mother brings them pine shoots to eat. Soon they can go farther from the drey and find food for themselves. One young squirrel tries to build his own drey. He doesn't notice a pine marten about to attack.

The marten pounces. As the squirrel leaps away he feels the animal's claws slide through his tail. He races from branch to branch but the marten follows. The squirrel makes a huge, wild leap across a gap.

He almost feels he is flying. He lands on branches that are too thin to hold the heavy body of the marten. The squirrel is safe but he is too far from home to return. Now he really has to build a drey.

Summer passes. The young squirrels learn how to strip bark and crack nuts. In autumn the forest is full of food and the squirrels grow strong and fat.

They bury some nuts, one at a time, to eat in the winter. The field mice also store food, but they bury lots of nuts in one hole.

The days get colder. The young squirrels have all left their mother now and built their own dreys. The mother squirrel builds a new drey too, between a branch and the trunk where the winter winds will not blow it away.

Fallen leaves and pine needles cover the ground and soon the snow will come. But there will always be pine cones for the squirrels to eat and under the ground is their store of nuts to see them through the winter.

More About Squirrels

The squirrel in this story is a red squirrel. It lives in coniferous trees and only comes down to the ground to find food. The smallest tree squirrels are the pygmy squirrels. They live in Africa and Asia and are no bigger than mice. The largest squirrels are the size of cats and live in India and Malaya. All squirrels can leap from branch to branch, but the flying squirrel has a flap of skin between its back and front legs and can glide a long way.

Grey squirrels are tree squirrels too. They originally came from North America but are now found all over Europe. They are bigger than red squirrels and live in all kinds of trees.

Ears: The squirrel has very good hearing

Tail: This helps the squirrel to steer and balance as it leaps. It acts like a parachute to slow its fall as it drops to the ground

Eyes: Large eyes help the squirrel to watch out for enemies all around

Whiskers: These help the squirrel to feel its way

Claws: These are sharp and curved for climbing trees

23

Some Special Words

Acorn The seed of the oak tree. This small nut has a hard cup at one end.

Coniferous tree A tree whose seeds are carried in cones. Most are evergreen trees and do not drop their leaves in autumn.

Drey A squirrel's nest. It is made of twigs and bark and shaped like a ball. It has no entrance – the squirrel just pushes its way in through the loose twigs.

Kitten A baby squirrel. Kittens begin to see and hear five days after they are born and their fur starts to grow at eight days. Three kittens are usually born together.

Pine marten A furry animal about twice as big as a squirrel. It lives in woods, particularly pine forests and feeds on small birds, squirrels and mice.

Starling A common bird which nests in trees or on the ground.